David Steingass | *Hunt & Gather*

David Steingass

Hunt & Gather

Poems New and Selected

1968-2016

*For Jim Lenfestey author of
"A Man in Love with Jackpine"*

David Steingass

9/17/18

Red Dragonfly Press

ISBN 978-1-945063-09-1

Library of Congress Control Number: 2016957577

Full acknowledgments printed at the back of the book

Cover design by Earl Madden

Author's photo by Brent Nicastro

Text set using Dante MT Std by Scott King

Published by Red Dragonfly Press
    P. O. Box 98
    Northfield, MN 55057
    www.reddragonflypress.org

CONTENTS

PART ONE: SELECTED POEMS

from *Body Compass*, 1968
The Poet Plays the Outpost Circuit 15
Midwest U.F.O 16
TV Reports of Vietnam 18

from *American Handbook*, 1973
Blizzard! 21
Realizing What Has Passed 22
The American Porch 24

from *New Roads, Old Towns*, 1988, and *Ratter*, 1990
Ratter 27
Smalltowns 28
River 29
Pig History 30
Ben Morris's Handful of Snakes 32
Black Walnut Stew 33
Buffalo Hunter 34
By Greyhound Window 35

from *Fishing for Dynamite*, 1998
Making Poetry Pay 39
Fishing for Dynamite 40
Learning the Dialect 41
Eating Religion 43
Riding the Moon-Pig 44
Trying to Understand the Party Line 45
Fishing in the Dark 47

Sweating through Sports 48
Pitching Horseshoes 50
Touching the Inland Shore 51
Looking where Turtles Point 52
Hugging A President Who Talks Tough 53
Bringing Home the Bacon 54
Dying, A Northern Pike Makes Us Shiver 55
Floating Toward the Bear 56

from *GreatPlains*, 2002
Bringing Back the Animals 59
Greta's Wail of GreatPlains Law 62
Seeds & Nests 63
The True Costume of GreatPlains 65

PART TWO: NEW POEMS

I

Bigfoot's Back In Town 71
What Farm Boys Say When they Have to Talk 73
Drunk on American Mythology 74
My Famous Classmate 76
Monster 78
Jung & Unafreud 79
Dreams-on-His-Skin 80
A Glimpse into the Old World 81
Stones and Poems Struggle to Agree 82

II

Up in Wisconsin 85
Woods Party Debate 86

Undressing the Scarecrow 87
Great Ghosts 88
New Orleans Parades 89
Photos That Hurt 90
Honeymoon 91

III

Renaming the Warblers 97
Long-Legged Birds on a Northern Pond At Dawn 98
Snapping Turtle 99
Midwest Café Dialog, with Dogs and Horses 100
Two Red-Bellied Woodpecker Tail Feathers 101
Animal Effigy Mounds 102
Photos of Alaskan Bears 103
Animal Mysteries 105

IV

Elsewhere in the Novel 109
Storms That Change Lives 110
Market Day in the Fairytale 111
Patience and Terror: An Oregon Trail Documentary 112
America's Century 115
Erratics 116
Something Human 117
Lost Photos of Crazy Horse 118
Nights When Everything Waits 119

V

Youth 123
Conspiracy 101 124
Porkbomb 125
Lives of the Ordinary Leaves 127

Two Consider Three, with Home, Love, Jim Beam, and
    Last Things   128
Rosemary in Clay Pots   129
Why I Love the P.O   130
One More Thing That Can't Be Said   131
Torn from History   132

Notes
Acknowledgements
About the Author

Dedication:

For creatures, places, and things
whose consciousness helped shape these poems

I

SELECTED POEMS

from *Body Compass*, 1968

THE POET PLAYS THE OUTPOST CIRCUIT

Dawn and dark are mirages
Falling into each other.
Traveling roughshod across the land,
Careful of spotted charts and compass,
I feel myself the first to see no trail
When I look back.

And what fierce brawling people,
Brooding on nothing for months of silence—
A walk, an offhand remark, a woman's eyes
In the lamp light exploding into blood
And broken bones.

Forces without form wait
Massive as the land.
And no one knows just where
The people disappear.

MIDWEST U.F.O.

She tosses,
One midnight so close the melons
Perspire on their loam,
And pitches stark awake in silence.
The clock's luminous fingers point
to a sprattled Readers' Digest
On the bed table, the county paper,
Her son's last letter
From the seminary in Wichita.
She touches it, her hands so milkhouse
Disinfectant-white they look
Sandblasted. She throws on the robe she sewed
With feed bag cloth, and hurries past
The lumped husband to an apple
Grove beside the house
Where she has come before.

It isn't lonely, she thinks, breaking
A twig, but only that the pastor
Comes each third Thursday for dinner.
An Ozark flight ponders overhead
Toward Pueblo. She knows the schedule.
There's not a light to see all night
And no other house by day.
She has memorized the Grange calendar.

Never on an airplane, never left the state.
The twig snaps in her hand. Planes take four
Hours all the way across. On tiptoe,

Breathing all she can hold, stretching
Three thousand miles, she feels twigs
Catch in her hair.

§ § §

A light like Christmas bulbs
Flickers inches from her nose.
The wind rises, blowing her hair, catching
Her robe. She runs at last as she has not
Run ever. The light twinkles, friendly, warm.

It says something she can hear
Almost, beyond the farm and darkness.
Beyond anything, beyond New York,
And only to herself. Perhaps to land
Another night, and speak. To look at her
As human, to hear her explanation first.
They know where things are friendly.

TV REPORTS OF VIETNAM

Some of them I knew, free
And lonely in the hills. We laughed
In summer.

      Now they swagger on film,
      Still lonely in their power.

      How do I take back my love
      Now their eyes are coal?

I would go to them with an arm
Around the shoulder again, saying
Friend of aspens and streams,
The weight of your boots, the squared
Thigh pockets make this happen,
The way things dangle from your belt
Making you change your walk,
What we saw together in the woods
And took into ourselves through different eyes.

from American Handbook, 1973

BLIZZARD!

"Wait it out at my place. Not
A serious walk." Denis Day, stockman,
Strolled offhand from Nebraska storm
To invite me.
                Gas tank empty, snow
A wind-thrown wall of darts, sleeping bag
A wet pelt across my back, I never saw his farm
Until I lost my car.
                His pickup slid
Across the Platte to clumps of herefords
And steaming calves, fur chips
Drifting through March. We wrapped one,
Fresh-licked, in burlap.
                It froze, blown
Open-eyed in the track's bed. All day
The head toppled on its twisted neck, chestnut eyes
Staring back. How can wind shriek
And echo through each cell? "Goes days,"
He said. "You miss her when she stops."
His rangy backbone of genes
Wound into door frame corners.
Even his belly slouched. He said nothing
More. Drank coffee, stared
At the windshield. Let me help
Carry the dead, and never
Asked my name.

REALIZING WHAT HAS PASSED

1

No one understands the film. Still,
Silent moments, how
The bullets strike. Frantic,
We yank a slide and blow it up—
Fail safe memory of one day
We all rode to Dallas in a black,

Open car. The wall clock's arms point, funnel,
And grind the fine powder of the stars
Closer to quicksilver.
Faces in the crowd contort, trying to realize
What the bullets are coming to.
Theirs are a fighter's nerves as his glass
Jaw begins to crack. Feather-delicate lobes
Take in the slug and bloom,
Atomically.

2

Before a portable black-and-white
With drifting vertical hold,
We crack a pop top
And watch the pole vaulter in the ad rise
Like a missile

To hover far beyond us. Up,
Out in the humming ice of space
The bullet approaches lunar docking
And the piston vaulter falls like a shot.
A hollow nosed tidal wave

Slams into the Sea of Tranquility.
Boot prints petrify on this
Eternal stare.

   3
In the end,
Our heads ache from just one beer
That afternoon bright as a bare bulb.
When the lights come on again
Years later, our slide brushes
The projector bulb to mushroom
Out of the picture.

Nothing eases the dynamic
Building up thinner that air.
Nobody knows anymore
What our travels found.

THE AMERICAN PORCH

Spread-eagle deck of an ark.
Its wooden swing chained from a stern heaven
Poses generations of black and white
Memory. The stiff lap sways like a metronome
Through Sunday double-headers,
Moves on any breeze
As though someone has just left
To shuck corn for supper, or strike sparks
Of dust between horseshoes stakes.
Or set out for work
On the sudden Monday morning of
The twentieth century, down the road that wound

Through bees in elderberries.
Before the bend of those huge,
Silent afternoons, you could look back
Where percale curtains hung listless as carp
Out the kitchen window. Frizzled at the gills,
A patriarch blue spruce shook
Hands over the rail as everyone dozed
And thought they dreamed.
                              You
Never return. Chances are malaria
Got you, or a war bride. The anchor
Half of the century flowers
To atomic proportions. Imagine, pygmies
Shrink your skull to essential size
And sew your lips shut.

from *New Roads, Old Towns*, 1988
and *Ratter*, 1990

RATTER

Black, bazooka-sleek spaniel,
the ratter rifled silos and corn shocks,
thrashing lumps from dusty straw and bombing

rats out of drain pipes and feed barrels.
Her ears the size of beef livers caught country
miles of code through hay bunkers

and root cellars. Where rats blurred the air
dim with furry electric arc leaps,
she raced to shake them harder

than I could watch, and crush their bone to bags
of damp sliver and brad. She piled sixty
rats dead one Saturday in

Mother's Hawkeye snapshot. Most violent
of our dogs who fell poisoned, run down,
or shot, she whimpered blind,

twitching her feet and moaning
through sleep after each
rat she dreamed back.

SMALLTOWNS

Isn't it little towns we love
            we end up running from? Places
                    who want us to come as we hope

we never were, and like enough we hold
            nothing back? We feel them push us
                    bigger than we think we'll grow

all the days they dog us,
            standing so close in elm shadow
                    we feel ourselves walk away from life

we understand we can't live up to. Faces
            people lug off the bus from Buffalo
                    Drop, or Cut-&-Shoot,

pack in each eye all
            they keep loaded and cocked
                    for life. Towns they left for dead

we catch them talking
            back to. Echoes that stare for years
                out of any mirror.

RIVER

Always the outback,
the upper neck's far unknown reach, the ear lobes sleek
as tiny fish holding breath.
In their skeins the lungs, two more fish, lounge
like the far slopes of

Nebraska. How fish lose themselves, lovely in wilderness
but lovelier still splashing light,
you can't imagine let alone understand
until you crouch at the river's edge
and feel the world arc

beyond your hand. Her bones braid
the way flesh meets itself to show where
she hides the earth. But never how. Even when you feel
her
breath catch still as skin,
it's always the same.

PIG HISTORY

Oh, porkers!
Substantial in your Sunday names,
you Berk, Duroc, and Yorkshire
brotherhoods. You geographic trick of Poland
China. You everyday Chester White
and Tamworth, all well-hocked
world travelers. Hampshire,
reliable as holidays in Easter egg-
banded hides. History is gold dust-
filled potato sacks, your manner says.
Pass through this pig's ear.

Oh, federation of
choice cuts! Snort to curlicue,
your heads cure as cheese, your feet
pickles. Your tails simmer into mock
turtle soup, your hair stands for tooth
and paint brushes. Your blood flows through sausage
veins in second life. Leaf-lard falls and burns
to boil the season your trunks split,
rustle, and knot your skin
like pretzels. You sail into dawn as bacon
boomerangs skidding on tiptoe
to bless breakfast.

Oh, solid citizens
to the end. Your clean-shaven lives,
the neutral corners you choose to shit,
each rending squeal you hold, and hold back
if held by only one leg. Your cuticles

pink as the day you kicked
free from the swampy womb
clear to your snout's blunt,
nearsighted grasp. How earnestly you love
the world. We hum the tunes our teeth grind
and taste in each bite the stew
earth cures as history.

BEN MORRIS'S HANDFUL OF SNAKES

Ben heard snakes slither
anywhere. He said this one bit
its tail to make a hoop and rolled,
tearing through brush like a stray
tractor wheel. Not even farm dogs
chased it. And some snakes stalk you,
he said. Snake's the whole smell of a pond,
where you kiss your ass goodbye. They can't bite
under water's the only thing that
saves you. But they slip into knots when they breed
you take for tangled water weeds
and flop through, he said. Then they slice
the surface and spit you dead,
straight in the eye from the far side
of nightmare.
     We shot snakes
where their bodies stitched creek beds like slivers
heat lightning itches. If you managed to kill one,
it didn't stay dead—more loops and squiggles than
water hose heaven. Even if pigs' forked toes tore,
and their sleeves of knuckled snout shot
snakes out of sight, they'd drop from willows
tonight where you walk, spinning out of air like leech
necklaces. Once when I reached for a jar of watermelon
pickles on the dark cellar shelf I felt coils
curl in the dim light. Anywhere Ben pointed,
my stomach churned, my knees knocked
loose and weak. He made my spine squirm
fresh legends whenever
he hissed *Snake!*

BLACK WALNUT STEW

The old farmers said poison. Even pigs
left walnuts lay. Where they slammed earth,
a smell harsh as garlic festered grass

to bile. When I scratched a black
walnut husk, the juice stung my nails
bitter and alive. No dialect rubbed

closer to the bone. No pig butchered
lard-smooth and hung still
as a dream in the walnut tree

was harder to understand. Walnut
stew quickened my life
where everything swam.

BUFFALO HUNTER

The brown rivers of buffalo shook
rattlesnake weeds beside our fires. Days on end
we shot the buff as Sheridan said
we must. They throbbed

under our knives like
heat waves shimmer. I dream of peeling
greasy hides we piled
higher than boxcars. Each day

their ruined skeletons float
the prairie—shiny skulls and ghostly
ribcages. Too hot to hold,
my rifle barrel steamed

where it fell. I won't chew blood
again. Last buff I saw leaned, like a tombstone
his big-as-a-teepee hide
tried to conceal.

BY GREYHOUND WINDOW

Now we ride down into snow.
Semaphore the sun throws on tombstones

shows a town with more graves
than people. Trees float in twilight,
farmsteads fling like dust a galaxy
abandons. All our lives we learn answers
to the wrong questions. A sudden
blindness today. Death's promise
firm as a handshake. A boy we pass

mucks out a shed, his furious eyes
the coals of winter stars
sunk into snow. Where he stands
anything's up that out of
loneliness. Each night leads to a cold ditch
at one edge of the attic bed in
his father's house. When he prays

his breath turns steel at tooth edge
to frost the blue air.

from *Fishing for Dynamite*, 1998

MAKING POETRY PAY

Here's a poem to pay the bills
& close deals with no bad feelings.
It settles for every cent you're worth
& not a penny less.

This poem drains the pasta
& redirects robo calls to the clowns
who cut you off in traffic.
It scratches your back

takes your hand when you're scared
throws off the fantods when you're crazy
holds your calls & generally
saves your ass.

It sits with you when you can't sleep
herds the owl of fortune to your shoulder
shoos the wolf out of the back yard
& rejections from your door step.

It's a poem that grows ever more
pliable as you touch. Its shape
holds a terrapin shell's burnished
intricate glaze & drifts

clear & clean from wherever
your life flows. Whatever you think it can't bear
curls with a guitar's whisper
& zest in each line.

FISHING FOR DYNAMITE

My first ocean swell,
age ten. Cross-legged on the deck of Jet-
the-percheron's back, I saw the sky dip and roll,
and Silver lurch like an iceberg
in harness. Jet&Silver—fur boats with full sails.

Giddy as a colt, Silver's pony keg-hooves,
his jumpy, stiff-legged dance. Jet
an easy drift, a compost muscle churned,
a deep thrum pulsing the full ship's hold.
Silver&Jet, their harness a ship's rigging

cunningly strung to rip the earth from orbits
ground in space. I felt fish pull through the reins,
big fish that struck like dynamite.
Their steel roots, rough bark, and stone.
Their fur-creaking grace.

LEARNING THE DIALECT

We hung horse harness in trees,
or let it collapse each day—
dark skeletons in the grass
where horses rolled. Clotting their sweat-frothed hides
in dust, they lurched to drown the world
with bellyfuls of iridescent
crumble-foamed piss.
                         All the rest was learning
to call the world five nicknames. Seasons—
habits earth repeats—
wove my senses. Tanagers fanned sparks
light struck in their tinder.
Piglets washed like wet stones
from the womb. Scythes tolled *half-dead,*
half-live. Their damp swish felled grass
sun steamed to hay. I smelled wild mint,
burdock and bulrush crunch
to musty slush, watched willow's hoof-
stripped inner bark ooze.
I inched into woods on green ladder rungs
leaf by various leaf. Each step shoveled coal
sand snow and gravel into fifty-seven acres of Geauga
County Ohio

dirt. I worshipped feathers and stones, wasp
and puffball citadels, the darts
hummingbirds quiver into blossoms.
I caught animals' eyes, their delicate webs
of tongue and nose, the fragile world
a two-headed toad's skin left

whole in the tractor's tread.
A baby possum bared her teeth
But let me lose my fingers
in her fur-lined pouch. I loved knots
and splicing, the plain histories dirt wove
through my toes, turtle shells and snake skins
filling my hands. I held so still
shadows climbed the air to ride
my shoulders. I knew I'd grow
into a tree. My limbs would hold the sun
long enough to turn
spectacular.

EATING RELIGION

Good and plenty, wind whispers,
such as there is. Farm kids know in their bones
whatever religion is, there's food
involved.
        Biscuit puffballs swell
kids into blossom. Ham steak halos
make them gleam like beech bark
in rain. Dumplings bounce down spiral
stairs of their ribs and omelets
fluff their bellies. Leaf lard bubbles
leaves of dough into powdered
sugar desert that foams
the kids' lips.
Taste the earth, they hear
in the strawberry patch-wilderness
toads and turtles tumble. A belched chorus
blesses everyone. Eat so nothing
spoils. Waste, the only sin
hulks eternally close.

RIDING THE MOON-PIG

I felt the sledge drive
through my knees. The pig
may have heard Grandfather's prayer
as the drumclap struck
between his eyes. His steaming blood
spilled a map to nowhere
I knew.
            The pig rose gleaming
sleek as a ship's prow
out of a scalding cauldron
the way half moons hung above
the barn. The nested cord fell
from its belly cavern—
a ghostly rope looped
to the sky's trap door. I lugged
the head by its ears,
poking dragon teeth. "The bride's
prize," Grandmother said.
Her shriek and gnarled laugh
danced along my skin and stood
my hair on end.

Guided by bloody charts
that drip as I walk, my dreams lead
the way. I raise the anchor
by sausage rope. *The Moon-Pig*
shivers in wind from the cold
side of the barn. I'm lost in
thick gooseflesh. The orders cannot
be read before dawn.

TRYING TO UNDERSTAND THE PARTY LINE

When she spoke telephone
I felt reception crawl across the bed
of my hand and up my arm
to coil snug in my ear the fantasy
she wove by party line.

Silos outside the window
stood like three sisters kicked
out of breakfast. Deep in the wire
I felt her muscle shiver, and her skin's
tongue-soft dialect hum a sound

my hands prayed to touch, pore
by steamy pore. I heard Elvis swirl
on her turntable. I smelled my prom gardenia
giddy in her skin-warm scent
crinkle electrically as she hitched

one foot all the way up
to take everything off.
Elvis tried to talk sexy but spun
dizzy. My stomach floated like moonlight
along telephone wires

that swallowed Planet Earth
without a ripple. Silence, the second language
she gave new life, licked its chops,
drenching my body in lymph and tight
pause. I felt her pout, the quick way sun

zeroed in a silo's hair trigger. Filled with longing
remote as starlight, I watched
the phone cord's stiff noose
flop. How could I go on now with all
I thought at last I understood.

FISHING IN THE DARK

Deep in the mulberry trees, my car hung
in curtains of humid air that dripped
like a wet net. My girlfriend roiled the plush
back seat like a fish splashing
pools of moonlight into shattering

glass. My lips felt a line tug
in her neck as her breath hooked
my ear. Her skin held me so tight
I felt myself drown in her Windsong.
Glossy as the lapful of minnows

the prince shivered under in his Grimm
Brothers story, I felt my breath slip
off its feet. Mercy, I lied, which
way, America? Anywhere,
I thought I heard. Forever.

SWEATING THROUGH SPORTS

Those days we pulled up our pants
both legs at once. Nothing kept us in bounds
or out of action. We passed up safe bets
and sure things, living so close
to the bone we ran wild
on pure sweat.

We trapped kneecaps and cracked back
what shot the gap, picking blind spots
out of the blitz, spurning the fair catch.
Tearing through bad film, we made plays
That trusted our hot sweat to patch
any field we broke.

We got game. Broke fast,
flew free, and called in special
delivery from downtown. Got up to slam
and pull down, living in the paint
where double-doubles paid
the price of our sweat.

Checked, we sprawled where net cords
wove crosshairs. Pucks bare-knuckled the crease
to zero in like bats. Slap shots slammed
the cage blunt as guilt
where sweat steamed our lives
numb.

We took pitches that found ways
to short hop our pinched

nerves. Curves we changed to sneak
through back doors hung high
and lived to haunt us. Sweat averaged each
error into the mix.

We thought our bull's eyes
would add up huge in the end with big
numbers in front. Bull's eyes that spun us
dizzy, spiraling to skunk egg-
zeroes the last day our sweat
left us cold.

PITCHING HORSESHOES

We toss your new life
from the far end of work. We dug all day,
piled and lugged, raked and burned
for this last chance to spin steel

we loop through air in barefoot
arcs. We want nothing more
than a chance to strike sparks
on horseshoes stakes. We want the light

shoes snare on their snaky ways
through dusty grass. We lift
and throw everything away
we cannot wait to find again.

TOUCHING THE INLAND SHORE

Milwaukee to Bloomington. *Open the window*
at American Maize, you said. *Breathe*
the way my old man smelled. I apologize,
stealing your father. He becomes
more and more important,

you'll see. Here's mine at the crosscut's
far end, the give-and-take, push-
and-pull through oak or maple still
unresolved between us.
Feel the drag, the whine of song

ol' misery whip smells
in the tree that hides you. Humidity steeps
the inland shore, ferments air it whips
thick as blood. Once tree crowns rip
the sky and lean to slug earth,

your heart skips. Surprised you survive,
you feel the earth try to move
for stampedes of tree trunk lumbering
through brush. Groans flow the dark hold,
the swaying sea of masts your land-looker

grandfathers cruised. You hear the night brood,
itching a trail your skin begins to
recognize. Who tells more? Which father knows
that place his feet fall
marks him home?

LOOKING WHERE TURTLES POINT

The great turtles mount each other like rocks
piled on canyon rims. *Galapagos*,
they scrape. *Galapagos*, the rhythm grates
a heavy ecstasy. In the shrine

his drool casts, I smell
alluvial stew. I try to see the eel
she swims in his mind. When she leaves,
he stands the way we all spend

high school. Poised by glacier,
paralyzed by indecision,
we try to guess which way the wind growls
its evolution of emotion.

HUGGING A PRESIDENT WHO TALKS TOUGH

Watch him slide away from the hard
questions. When his wish to kick serious butt
springs him through the TV screen
where you sit taking your beer, tell him you're glad

he's come where you can hug him
like he deserves. Mention his rank
in your lineup of guys life's too short
to humor. Show him the look you polish

for rush hour. Ask him do Marines come for supper
at his place? Their lightning-slick swords,
their eyes lit with blood? Or the secret service playing
its friendly game of guns-for-bucks? Prod.

Bring up hillbilly lyrics he says he loves
that ring flat when life calls home
collect. Watch the child glare from his gene pool,
battery acid furious in each eye.

Feel your body grow warm in places
his part counts nothing. Rattle
your sword. Feel the tune it strikes up shake
each of your joints free at last.

BRINGING HOME THE BACON

Make a list for the store. You could forget why you've come if you don't, or even who you are once you're here. Ball points say *elite*. Fountain pens shout *anathema*, like stray car alarms. Use a blunt-as-your-heel kid's pencil with no eraser (there's no turning back). Writing words like *anchovy*, *primavera*, or even *bucatini*, you feel your sweat break hot. Pause then. Breathe a last safe breath before box cutters begin chopping into the frozen

pizza. Consider Wonder Bread's tract mentality that strands what it touches in the burbs. Resolve to avoid what's processed and salvage your dreams. Revel in the nugget-y smell and touch of organic oats and wild rice you scoop, how they recall times you made love fully exposed. How exciting your vulnerability makes the cocktail hour! The wild dreams of youth that fill your sleep! Once endive chirps like happy virgins fluttering in chipped

ice, for instance, you cease forever to covet your neighbor's daughter. Feel yourself weep for the pure gold chances you spurned, and those rock-solid possibilities you've blown away. Consider these pickled mushrooms from Gourmet Foods. How they could as well have been magical French cheeses. Aren't you capable of breaking the bank like this always? Any time? Whisper this dream with all the best details you imagine to the tall

blonde you surprise flash dancing among the fresh sausage links. How your head swims amazed through her marbling! Will she fold under the pressure of the store? Or save your number to put you, when it matters, where you belong? Anything's possible. You could be found out during your next breath. Play your chances right for once. Jump in your car and peel out quick. This minute, while you still have a clue how to bring the bacon home.

DYING, A NORTHERN PIKE MAKES US SHIVER

Edges of his face shred the smut
dusting gun barrels, the smell rain
ferments in tin cans, the hair trigger-silence
prowling land mines. Wherever tables set

he's built to slide his ruthless
butcher-barge. Two last talents—lunge
and wrench—thud stark as Viking swords
just behind the door.

FLOATING TOWARD THE BEAR

Think of the child lost in your flesh,
how bear smell shambles his thought.
He can't understand the huge fur
he feels stretch in thickets and walk

big as the woods through your sleep.
Imagine he brings you the story tonight
he's known all your life—the bear
who knows we are deadly

but steps from shadow and bark
to hold your sleeve in his teeth.
All you've forgot led you here
where the woods still begin.

from *Great Plains*, 2002

BRINGING BACK THE ANIMALS

Native Son poked through the junkyard below Lovers Lane

> luminous clock faces & disembodied pool ball eyes
> pancaked shoes & baseball mitts worn thin as chance
> spangled loops tendrils spirals & whorls
> snapped-off ski bones sled runners & fishing poles
> corkscrewed bicycle frames & rusty corn knife blades
> translucent flakes iridescent opaques & exotic glitters

Centipedes sow bugs & mushrooms spronged out of squashed
      baking powder cans
Pebbley-backed toads thunked through leaves and snakes
      unwound to fly through grass heaven
He touched a smooth snake bed once astounded by its polished
      mosaic slate patio
Just as he began to feel the wind rattle across the prairie
   and slam back empty-handed to whine around his flank and
      slip
      through his fingers like the huge memory of buffalo

He grew sad the great bison shaggies no longer wandered as
      brown clouds
   to quiver grass blades and splash the dust

What about junkpiles of animal parts he began to think

> buffalo tongue & hide ridges
> bone & skull outcrops
> antler spirals & bear claw cones
> skeletons like gleaming cages of air

Sifting and touching them made his hands quiver as if they were
        dreaming

Crazy he thought how junkpile lopsides & moans touches &
        clicks
    jostled his head like a day full of echoes winding among
        anvil-shaped GreatPlains thunderheads

He speculated at least one imperfectly-formed creature scattered
        through every GreatPlains dump

Juggling mounds of stray parts & pieces he began to understand
the lesson of the junkpile that nothing survives whole is bitter
the way first snow flurries vanishing into the earth are bitter

beautiful
            but bitter

These new animals he vowed will have lifelong cricks and none
        of their ancestor's effortless throat-catching grace

He danced & clapped & proclaimed chapter & verse his voice
        rumbling among hills & clouds
I demand stone age ferociousness he said along with precision of
        emotion

All this happened slowly
Long walks on which he pictured giant femurs
Wandering meditations about the sound a stegosaurus makes
        whistling the anthems of the wind through its plates

Quiet times diagramming rustpelts shuffling & skidding before
      the immense barrage of GreatPlains wind

At last he saw the herds begin to rise dusty stiff on ill-fitting joints
thousands of misfits clanking the magnetism of loss & neglect
But mine Native Son said clicking his heels high
                                        MINE
His skin tingled watching a buffalo-rooster sway in its rickety
      crouch
feathers sprouting its hump a blood-red comb splitting the armed
      territory of its skull

Sit
      he told the first one

You will be called 3-legged
   Sagebrush-&-rust-clanking
      Morning-smelling GreatPlains Junke
                            and you &
you & you

Rusty pelts fumbled to their scaled hooves as far as he could watch
      them screech

He banged a sign into the mailbox pole Private
Purebred GreatPlains Breeding Stock
                        Breeding
Must Not Be Disturbed

This Means You

[signed] Native Son
Prop & Prog

GRETA'S WAIL OF GREATPLAINS LAW

My waterbed's an island
crawling with thigh-shaped legends
a GreatPlains way of life the dream
you wake from only with regret

That's too much too fast
forget where you're expected
Feel your hands wash over me
skin-side down to bedbone

I spin the compass Cha-Cha
What do you care the world turns flat
long as I'm round as far as I stretch
long as you drown in my noose

and your center jumps & runs out to dance
in the shallows of my island continent
What other home could your bones know
once my fingernails raze your skin

and I seal your lips by tongue
By sunset you'll sting and grow numb
happy to leash your life to the stars'
cold frenzy of loneliness and law

SEEDS & NESTS

Native Son nodded over a seed catalog full of okra mung bean
      radish & beet grenades
  and purple floodlights of flowering kale stroking lush-thighed
      eggplant's translucent snake pants

He'd felt something weird taking place on the prairie for months
      muttering twitches lip pursings & knuckle cracks
  buttercrunch crinkles as surprising as the sunsets everyone
      grew so solemn about

The castle's sod roof creaked & leered above him glistening with
      crawlies & slithers
  blackberry nests ground pine & cherry pungent as mashed
      walnuts & fermenting burdock

The catalog slumped from his hands

Waist-deep wading the GreatPlains Slough in muddy twilight
  he reached inside *GreatPlains grabbags of* snake holes & snapper
      dens dodging red-winged blackbirds shaking their fists and
      mocking him with guttural Cyrillic texts and saw marsh
      grass tips sketch the wind as though decoding messages
      crickets & cicadas spent their lives singing

He stared at the grass & damp roots until he felt snakeslip &
      cattail slide delicate lingerie of earth on & off & up along
      his spine
                not to mention down

He couldn't believe the ways he began to see nests throb &
      beckon
He'd never thought about them that way but why not
A nest is a net he realized
a safe house among marshes thumping with bulrushes' starchy
      beat tamarack & fern fingers jumping in place and
      catalpas' swollen thumbs

Everything flies he blinked for focus and felt his head spin before
      take-off
seeds into sycamore leaves green bats into furry butterflies and
      those fuzzy angels the hummingbirds
                                        vanish

      wherever I look

THE TRUE COSTUME OF GREATPLAINS

Fall in GreatPlains
The smell of damp leaves & burlap sprawled in the quiet shadow
        places
Autumn

The kind of late afternoon sun that sneaks through your clothes
        Native Son thought
rubs your back not getting too hot about it
and bubbles black walnuts out of their husks

The dangerous kind of sun that made him feel too happy with
        finding his way to Greta
                            and her Castle in GreatPlains

He slid into his white suit and splashed bay rum thinking of Greta
        climbing into herself the way a cat curls to sleep

The mayor of Aguas Caliente scurried in his inscrutable serape
        flapping
He'd just discovered that Native Son sent every gardenia in town
        to Greta
Woodsmoke the mayor said *smells close to cinnamon with a finish of
        GreatPlains sage*
Anything to keep this strange *Americano* engaged until the *Senorita*
        appeared

Native Son put his foot on the rail and remembered Greta
        swimming through her fur bikini
He tried to picture the century in which stone and redwood
        began

Hot springs and limes as sweet as oranges he thought handling
      his cigar as though it was a banderilla

A kid ran up to shine his shoes and ask for his autograph
Native Son pointed out geese drifting across GreatPlains
Everything waits to jump out at the right time he said feeling the bay
      rum begin to work
        wondering how the world seemed so fuzzy-edged & possible
        like the view through a quartz lens

They sat in the heat of the patio bar in the GreatPlains Palomar
Each of them mayor shoeshine boy & Native Son watched the
      ceiling fans circle like lazy helicopter blades
    and pictured Greta illuminate an upstairs room of their choice

Native Son felt as far away as the discovery of woven fibers like
      flax
He thought everything he could but nothing more than the
      burnish of Greta's hair like an animal's pelt
running it through two or three times until he thought he
      understood

He dropped his cigar in a potted banana plant and spit through
      the thicket of his beard
He could almost feel her hair rolling into pliable sycamore shoots
He considered her eyes seeing him and felt warm fish begin to
      drift through his blood
Eucalyptus in the wind spreads the history of Greta he murmured
      understanding the connection as she began to walk down
      the stairs
                dissolving the stone as she moved

II
NEW POEMS

1

BIGFOOT'S BACK IN TOWN!

> *These guys don't want to find Bigfoot—*
> *They want to be Bigfoot.*
> —Robert Michael Pyle, *Where Bigfoot Walks*

Life's so good in the land of the elk, the Dutch oven, and the fat
    grizzly,
  what brings him and six feet of diamondback rattler
    looping his neck like

castanets? Good question you forget once he struts like an oak
    trunk walking
  wrapped in bear and buffalo fur, daring you or any
    flatfoot try to disrespect

or diminish him. You should say: Where were you when I had to
    choose
  the fork in the trail, how many eons ago?
    Problem is, his hair's

better than yours—way, senator-grade better—down to each curl's
    glossy
  quiver. Forget that your scars don't show. Who cares
    that you can explain

each of your canines with a straight face? You can only stare at the
    juicy slab
  of mane and lick your lips as he yells *Let's sail away*
    in our skins! or *Child support's*

a plot! And when he shouts *Responsibility betrays carnivores!*
    his tone, his ivory tusks, and his roar's volume
        curdle your blood.

$ $ $

The louder he claims he's free,
    the more he starts to resemble your brother-in-law
        on opening day—as in, how many beers will he drain

before furniture
    starts to break. That's when he drops the nicknames
        you thought died in study hall. You feel their rusty grain

gnash your spine's
    chain of teeth. If your knees and elbows crack
        while he swaggers like a statue of the coach you've hated

all these years, invent
    any story to save you later in the *Dew Drop*
        Inn. Explain how no one knows karate if you get a good one

in first. Flash the smile
    made famous by your traffic finger as you wave
        your pure product of America white-knuckled goodbye.

WHAT FARM BOYS SAY WHEN THEY HAVE TO TALK

Given their druthers, farm boys skip the whole idea of speech. But if one has to talk—say the dentist wants to double check which tooth to pull—a farm boy still won't say *love*, the kind of word that dizzies him. Pull out his fingernails and he won't say *love* any more than admit night's strange power. "Could be," he'll nod. "Yeah." Sentences like these make up most of his conversation, especially if he gets caught alone with a woman he's unrelated to. Sooner or later she'll say something like "Doesn't tonight feel like a blanket to curl into?" "Depends," the farm boy chokes, stunned by her question. He feels the walls begin to pulse as the floor between his feet cracks open.

He moves from bedazzled to bedeviled in the time it takes maybe three of her sentences to *thunk* into the side of his head. If she'd ask about something he knows, like how many bales of first-crop hay to expect from each acre of clover, given the spring rain, maybe. But emotions? The kind of thing he'd go without supper to avoid? He stares out the kitchen window as though twilight announces a mutant invasion. His mind tugs like a big catfish. "Sure," he says, "whatever," while his heart tap dances through his chest. "You betcha," he elaborates. But no matter how much air he packs into his lungs, he feels his body begin to disintegrate into the black puzzle that is night.

"Gold in the Black Hills!" the young woman yelled and lurched like a freeway of rush hour traffic. She might have been General Custer in drag. Same exclamation point-voice, same big sky attitude that presents most dynamically in America. The race to fame flexes its wings, caught in the fairy tale kind of devotion FaceBook commands. Bugles sound the charge, twitter echoes the fury, and the stampeding bodies begin. It's easy to forget how much anybody's had to drink. Who keeps count? #don'twetwerkanychanceweget?

George Armstrong saw the disheveled victor face the pristine loser over the Appomattox treaty table. He rubbed President Lincoln's elbow riding horseback at dawn in Washington. He grew his hair long for ten years, dreaming of the Little Bighorn, and tailored his buckskin version of the cavalry uniform to resemble Natty Bumpo turned mountain man. Wasn't his docu-drama life based on real events made for his American moment? He rises out of dusty cowboy and Indian reruns still, his golden status as 19th century sit-down interview untarnished. Imagine the YouTubes, the sepia-lit Instagrams, the digital daydreams. Who'd bet against unknown Crazy Horse selfies floating around the aether the way Custer's doomed tweets reign viral in the frontier's echo chamber?

And who cares if he phoned-in the fight and stuck with Reno in the bluffs, or took his last bow in the afternoon dust with a tray of frozen daquaries. Ditto the claim he was teetotal. Fresh schemes download daily in America, shaken or stirred. Custer wasn't the first dry drunk who needed an audience to focus. Bravado and vulnerability fester in any personality the media marks, and

Custer had the golden boy's maddening bullet-proof persona that drew the press. Civil War battles that resembled Indian war massacres to come smoldered in his eyes where the American prowl for face time festers. So addictive is our conviction about the power of the last round knockout, the two-minute drill, and the sudden death victory that we call whatever happens golden if only it glimmers. When the opportunity stares from a mirror and the band strikes up "Gary Owen," the general's favorite march, who questions young women who rise to his occasion? Few of us can avoid taking our best, if wildest shots, hoping only that the chips gleam where they fall.

MY FAMOUS CLASSMATE

Famous, maybe, but first he was my high school classmate. He stalked around Oak Park in a Sherlock Holmes hat and lumberjack boots. Came back from the war with a cane and officer's cape with bullet holes he pushed his fingers through. That's his almost-smirk in black and white photos from the school annual. *Then what happened?* his expression always seemed to say. This's what you're after, the go-for-broke attitude, like in his story about the big fish? *Ernie*, everybody called him. *None more clever*, all the girls said.

Take the games we made up. We'd creep around barn rafters until we dove or fell into the haymow. How much could hay hurt? he shrugged. We even threw ourselves down flights of stairs. Mostly wood, but stairs. Show me who can't stand up to a staircase? he said, like there was an answer. Everything we played was homemade, and full of sixteen-year-old double-dares. Stuff you paid for when you lost. I learned to dread his fists. He slugged your shoulder, and red hot goose eggs popped up quick!

We fought only once, while pressing apples for cider. All afternoon the *must* of apple seeds and skins gathered in the bed of the press as the juice drained off. Pressing apples was harder than you might imagine—wood machines, of course, that cranked by hand. Try crushing an apple in your bare hands. Anyway, we got sweaty and flushed, and I saw that something was digging at him. "Lady lips," I heard him whisper, and caught the look in his eye. And because I was sixteen the same year I said, "Your mother's kisses."

He was on me like snow off a steep roof—an avalanche of elbows, knees, and head butts. I knew his mother only because she made us blueberry grunt once, up in Michigan. But when I read how Krebs's mother made him kneel and pray with her, I remembered the way his mother said the word *grunt*. I still see his face after we rolled around in that sweat-churned dirt. The look in his eyes made me wonder, that day to this. The fight seemed strange to me then and even stranger later, since he was always so big on control.

MONSTER

I want your children.
I want to eat your heart.
      —Mike Tyson

He punches so hard,
wooden chairs we sit on jump.
His shoulder blades' scorpion dance
scrawls the air and climbs the wall
we lean against. Our pulses slam

like metal gates as we wash
the blood from gravestones
standing up in our dreams. However
we scrub, blood seeps back
and the stains remain.

JUNG AND UNAFREUD

"He had the tiny feet?" she said. "Betcha." Something about her eyes took my head off just above the ears. "Summers barefoot," she said, "and ordinary things would not have scandalized him."

"Ease up," I said. "He died of throat cancer." "I thought that was the other one," she said. "The shadow-guy." I watched her hair keep the rhythm of her voice. "Anyway. Today it would be private jets to Hollywood from his Sedona clinic."

"And what about those taproot-cigars they puffed around on?" Her voice meant to gnaw on this glittering shard. "What's not to say!" she insisted. "I mean, really? You explain him better?"

DREAMS-ON-HIS-SKIN

(After *Prize Bull*, by H. Call, 1876, National Gallery of Art)

Born too late to travel with Lewis and Clark, Hannah Call is hired to paint children, or animals like this farmer's bull in its New York farm meadow. She'd like to title her painting the way American Indians call children after character traits, or dreams, or weather. Their inner, strange, psychic names. She knows the story of Sacagawea and her daughter Janey—girls on The Expedition. She knows Karl Bodmer's Mandan Indian portraits, also Mr. George Catlin's Missouri River paintings. And she knows how to cloak this lunk of a bull in feathered boas and fiddlehead swirls until he resembles designs she's seen in pictures of Four Bear's robe, or the body painting of He-Who-Makes-the-Path, both chiefs in their tribes.

When she steps back from the easel there's a line of sinewy red clouds edging into sight in the western sky. *Stealthy,* she thinks. *Delicate.* She feels her pulse jump, as it did when she read newspaper accounts of General Custer's fate on the Little Big Horn River. Today, July 12, 1876, is a humid Wednesday morning almost twenty days, she calculates, since the newspaper reported "massacre." *Yes,* she decides. She'll paint the blood-stained clouds into her picture. Squire Adolph-of-the-bull said nothing about her fur inventions yesterday. What would make him notice these clouds this morning? She works on, feeling the hair on her forearms stand like secret Indian knowledge of buffalo bones and joints.

A GLIMPSE INTO THE OLD WORLD

Crows swagger in the snow. They look like a gang of Isaac Babel's drunk cavalry officers as they peck the skull of a paper wasp nest into confetti. Log hovels burn soundlessly in winter dawn's light. Carcasses twist in the snow. "To Whom It May Concern," blown and torn notes begin. "Dearest." Unsheathed beaks drip slate-colored blood. Europe smolders everywhere.

What's to drink? an officer growls. Other men stare into the ashes.

Years later at the reenactment, the old grizzlies drain bottles until they begin to quarrel. Each man claims he drank the most vodka on those long-ago raids they can barely remember. Loud voices disagree about where Max stood before he vanished. What made him blow his career that day requires even more bottles. Shoving commences. Cursing begins. Duels seem inescapable.

STONES AND POEMS STRUGGLE TO AGREE

Sifted out of backfield glacial quarries by color
texture and face to rearrange
in patchwork walls by the mind's ceaseless
      feng shui

    Poor Herman (Mrs. Melville said)
    He wrote a book about fish no one wants to publish
    Now he's gone back to poetry

      The pencil lead's wet dirt smell
      its shifting point and its willingness
      to give everything away—all of which
         concerns a stone in what way

2

UP IN WISCONSIN

We drink *Sex on the Beach* in a barn gussied-up for tourists. Talk clanks through the cow stanchions. "Imagine," she smiles.

> *Want my green olive? They taste like silage smells.*
> *She's embarrassed she can singe a goose?*
> *I give her a couple shots. She's up there nice and clean.*

I watch her tongue slice the light. "You dress as though you have strange thoughts," she says. "It's not that kind of place?" I ask.

> *Best birth control is the apple.*
> *I'll bite. Before or after?*
> *Instead.*

"*Seen your dog inna zoo,*" I say again to make her laugh. "There's a better place for underwater plumbing?" she asks. Twilight jingles like a sack of silver dollars.

> *You find us, I sez. Yer the cop.*
> *Your puppy tongue looks like a geranium petal.*
> *Go lay onna grass, I told him, you wanna act like a dog turd.*

"More drinks with little umbrellas," I say. The waiter's fingers burn when he picks up her glass.

WOODS PARTY DEBATE

My girlfriend's hair smells of wild
mushrooms and lush Bulgarian
thyme. Falling leaves splash our blanket
they wash away into a desert
island. Canada geese with flight caps

knotted under their sleek chins
spot us. *Can law school meet
our needs?* they argue as they plop
like milkweed pods in the pond
to listen. I ask the lovely Sofia, *Why*

hold back now? Her swamp water-
dark eyes glitter, her smoky
freckles and rain-slick
deviled eggs alive with Cyrillic
tendencies. Stunned,

the geese bob and freeze
where they float. *Cloudy,* mourning doves warn.
Overcast, the crows add. This stage of deliberation,
each word sounds more risky than
anything that's come before.

UNDRESSING THE SCARECROW

Her clothes tug like cotton candy

down to the wire and duck
tape in Freda Kahlo's *Broken Column.*
                              Can we stop
pretending? she says, her voice everything high school
warned about. *Depends,* wind's loose hand
slides, *how many nights we have.*
                              Some women don't know
their strength, how their eyes chip flame
wherever their glances fall.
                              Hers broke loose
like a horse racing back
to the fiery barn.
                    Lest you forget bubble gum's
first wild taste, she said, spitting
in the wind's eye. *See where*

I'm headed here?

GREAT GHOSTS

Luna moths wander up the porch steps on hot June nights and bump against the lighted screens. Nothing about them seems to fit the night. Their wings seem too big to be real, like disembodied dinosaur skins fluttering the heart-skipping colors of bone, sperm, and longing. The sound is close to western movies unreeling in small town film projection booths. The more the moth wings move, in fact, the more they resemble sagas of prairie schooners filled with the kind of desperation that depends on failed communication. Forget plans, wagon wheels whisper as they slice the brittle-crusted desert sand. Talk had as little chance on the way west as anywhere, luna wings seem to agree. You might be surprised at what pioneers were willing to forget, they continue. Why they left home, to begin with. A dusty sense of risk and exposure must have hovered over the wagon trains—a texture that clung to the roof of every mouth. In time, pioneers may hardly have remembered things like speech, clinging instead to what seemed more promising, more immediate. Especially spectral on nights like this, luna moth wings seem both tenuous and clingingly insistent, like other great ghosts of desire.

NEW ORLEANS PARADES

Mardi Gras lasts all week. A parade called The Boy Who Won't Play Fair runs constantly. No More Lunatic Republicans Forever is also a favorite. The worn and dented brass guts of The Society for Our Dear Friends Dead of AIDS pile as musical instruments on the sidewalk outside Harry's Corner at two-fifteen Monday mornings while the pre-march toast happens inside. New Orleans parades average one every three days all year. The Girl Who Got Away appears in brunette, redhead, and *Jolie Blon* plumeage. The version with kinked Orphan Annie-hair twirls strings of plastic beads from the third storey deck of her St. Patty's Day float. Afternoon sun works its beat-down magic. The strings settle like nooses around necks stunned by the bare-fanged spectacle. Irish potatoes and cabbages along with blood's mixed intentions hammer skulls. By the time the girls show their Spanish onions, your bare feet float like mandolin notes along flagstone paths in the cool courtyards of your mind. In the distance, an ocean liner's orchestra strikes up fox trots for patrons in stiff patent leather shoes. Their fresh white shirts flash too bright to watch in the sunlight. The crew lowers life boats into the icy sea. The crowd applauds like spontaneous combustion as the ship dodges icebergs. The orchestra sounds ready to appear each second around the corner where you keep watch.

PHOTOS THAT HURT

You don't mean the camera's angle
that shows your poor technique. It's the eight
by ten glossy of the girl who talks
the way running water ripples

that wounds you bone-deep.
Her slipknot of smile, the way her face holds
light that blinds your memory.
Her trick of touching thought

while you think. You feel your face
you made perfect just for her
flop away awkwardly for
everyone to see. This photo,

you mean. Her bare skin's victory
glaze. Its dazzle of razor
sharp teeth she prays
you won't feel in time.

HONEYMOON

The groom forgot to make sleeping car reservations, so the honeymoon begins in a Spirit of New Orleans coach car creeping out of Chicago with what's left of the wedding cake tucked under the bride's seat. When the train groans to a stop in Cape Girardeau, the groom's confidence quivers again. Once the night falls apart, what's to say to this woman he barely knows he finds himself alone with?

The bride imagines New Orleans just below Chicago one stop after Memphis. Cape Girardeau reminds her of big parking lots in the east. The wind shifts southeast by dawn, bringing the smell of Ella's Café through an open window. The newlyweds wander across the tracks against the conductor's advice for their first married breakfast. The groom falls into conversation with girdle salesmen bound for a convention in Memphis. The bride sees that the menu offers no fresh strawberries which she associates with successful restaurant tables. She watches her husband shake catsup over his potatoes. No one in her family eats potatoes, which equal horse fodder in Russian villages. But she loves the way he says *homefry*. The train whistles three times. Husband and wife look at each other, possibly for the first time. He needs a shave, she realizes, a situation up with which she should not put. She resolves that never again will her hair behave the way it does today.

Salesmen slide into their booth. One man snaps a rubber band on his wrist. "Who doesn't want efficient?" he says, talking to the groom, winking at the bride. All her life she's seen men forget themselves over money and business. Another salesman watches her stir cream. Her hand excites him. She feels his knee against her thigh. His sweat's smell makes her realize she'd choose death before she'd agree to wear a girdle, a decision she's happy to express. Girdles bring Amy Lowell to mind, *The Bride Comes to Yellow Sky*, and cities like Enid and Buffalo. The groom remembers a girlfriend who told a joke about garter belts, how they held something as they gave something else away. He remembers how she knew her way around garter belts. The salesman imagines the bride licking wedding cake frosting. When the train whistles again, the salesman's breath catches somewhere in the flood of the bride's lilac bath water fragrance. She remembers that she and her husband share a birthday, and feels herself shiver despite the humidity.

Questions. Use whatever you need from the narrative to discuss:

1. Salesmen. How many laid end to end make a good story?
2. Stories. (a) How does the husband alter his former girlfriend's joke? (b) What will the salesman tell his wife about the bride?
3. Condiments. What part will catsup play in the bride's life? How will fresh strawberries influence which way the groom's wind blows?
4. Statistics. One-third of girdle salesmen's combined worldliness equals what portion of newlywed self-consciousness? How does the factor of gullibility apply?
5. Details. What memory will each newlywed keep of today's: (a) Train smell, (b) Small town dialects, (c) Salesmen, (d) Conductor, (e) Scenery?
6. Speculation I. How many train whistles must the bride hear before she (a) learns to sing along or (b) understands?
7. Speculation II. What is bath water?

8. Consequences. If the train leaves the newlyweds in Ella's Cafe, what are their chances? If they make it back to the train before it leaves, what are their chances?
9. Extra credit: Interpretation. How does the groom's memory change the story? Describe the wedding cake frosting the salesman imagines the bride licking. Why does she shiver?

3

RENAMING THE WARBLERS

Slate-sided yellow-rumped worm-
eating chats. Who chose such flat
syllables? Blue-wing. Black-throated green.
Pine, Olive, Black-and-white. Dust
collects in every corner
of these names.

We need more Prothontary, Magnolia,
and Cerulian. Their tails flip once,
and you hear Blossom
Dearie sing: *Throat-catch,*
Flip-flop, Whippersnood,
Stun.

Her little jazz bird's eighth
note-throb picks out hot
pepper sparks a wing tip flicks
the way sun finds glass
in gravel. And drags them
sideways through the air.

LONG-LEGGED BIRDS IN A NORTHERN POND AT DAWN

Blue herons stand like fastidious butchers in long aprons as they throw down breakfast plates of ham and eggs. *More Schopenhauer,* they mutter through stogie smoke's fluttering visions of old girl friends. *Ditto Nietzsche. We'd still find tail feathers tucked behind our ears.*

Moody traveling companions, each bird thinks of his fellows knee-deep in shadowy water. *World as will and idea,* indeed! Each bird knows someone who wouldn't last a day without ginger schnapps.

What is it that you do? nieces at the heronry ask, though they're not sure they want to know. *Crosswords,* the birds croak, pointing bills like clock hands, scrawny and foreboding. *The unseen world,* another elder adds. His neck moves like a furry snake.

SNAPPING TURTLE

Call him Mr. Snapper, Sir Hand-to-Hand, or Sergeant of the guard. Call him Uncle homeboy meat man if you want. But smile when you do. He's the raw-boned reason people around here lock their doors, his personality like a bale of barbwire dragging greasy plate mail through the swamp. People like what he does okay— the whole enforcer thing—they just don't want to watch him do it. Well, nobody likes him pissing off the front porch. But they really don't want to open a door and surprise him in the middle of something. Just like nobody admits knowing wherever he's from—somewhere to hell and gone in the middle of a swamp the map labels: *Here Be Monsters*. People squirm when he grins and especially when he drools. "Like I care," he growls through his snear. He's mayhem personified? Home invasion run amuck? Whatever's hideous. "We jolly him up?" people say, "won't he act the way he looks?"

MIDWEST CAFÉ DIALOG, WITH DOGS AND HORSES

"Bad luck with the wife." A voice like big toes stubbed on
        glottal stops.
"Ugh." Eyes like a dog's with wind in its ears.
"Waukie-Sconson?"
"Ugh."
"Can't ever count on 'em."
Bookend shrugs at opposite walls.

"Jeet yet?"
"Jew?"
"Cheatin' a-tall?"
"Gunta."
Strident voices—half challenge, half threat.

"Then let's."
"Ugh."

Talk like this breaks out, wild horses can't drag them apart.

TWO RED-BELLIED WOODPECKER TAIL FEATHERS

Don't be fooled by the name. These feathers shine black and
white like snow on charred wood. A single feather could be an
accident. Two feathers mean subterfuge, like a map torn in half.
Survivers at dawn, the feathers plan to live forever like the rocks
and the rain.

They resemble one-legged ladders at a cliff dweller site. The white
rungs flit like Venetian blinds. The black rungs glide like predator
fish through lie detector tests. *Try to live one day unamazed,* the
chill breath shivers. When the light shifts, blood stains show.

ANIMAL EFFIGY MOUNDS

How much dirt borne by hand and patted into mounds grew massive enough to shape into animal dream creatures? Geese soaring on spread dirt wings? Bears prowling like men in fur muttering secrets? Ohio's Great Serpent Mounds stretched in the spirit world sun. Cahokia sprawled across the river from St. Louis and up the Mississippi to the Trempealeau domes close to Aztalan Wisconsin picnic grounds. Traditional EarthArt must have been a high school major. Lightning bolts chopped into Roche a Cri State Park sandstone show power passing into humans by way of thunderbird wings.

Such a ruckus had to generate foreign interest. What kept the Iceman stuck in the Italian Alps thirty thousand years ago except the new medium of limestone cave painting? How to account for the string of turquoise beads he hid in Wisconsin graduate school's earthen mounds that stayed hidden? Wasn't the time ripe for a career-changing new world visit of discovery? His travel itinerary smoke signaled around his head all morning, dancing like heat lightning. He felt so excited, so light-headed in the mountain air that he never felt the fist of flint arrowhead *thonk* into his back.

PHOTOS OF ALASKAN BEARS

Chilkoot Pass, 1896

A rope stretches up through the Chilkoot Pass and out of snowy sight toward the gold fields. Men in bear fur coats as shaggy as John L. Sullivan's mustache cling to the rope. Because each man has to hump 800 pounds of supplies over the hill to prove his starch, the packs look big enough to hold sewing machines or even small pianos. One bundle is so ungainly it could conceal a dead horse. Snow to the horizon hides frozen mountains that hold a few grains of actual gold, the prize everyone's left home for.

Dark Angels

Black under their white angel robes, polar bears rise on trunks of hind legs into thirteen feet-high fur-covered towers. Native American mythology says bears often claim wives from groups of Indian girls picking berries on mountain slopes. Today's bear is a confirmed bachelor, however. He spends his thought on a Ripon Wisconsin log cabin where the Republican party began in 1848. He tries to imagine, and not for the first time, what would make *Ursus maritimus* join anything that morphed from Lincoln's blossom into a swamp creature shaped like a shrub.

Grizz

Who knows why this grizzly bear is so attracted to French mountaineers that he follows them into the Brooks Range? "What the hell," he tells himself. "Another century's coming. Try something new. The French are famous for unusual thoughts." Flurries of mosquitoes the size of bats rise out of the permafrost.

He draws so close the hikers recognize his blood-streaked pig's eyes. The bear remembers standing upright, walking like these hikers, once. Which doesn't mean he wants to do it again. But either way, he sniffs, the picnic's a fun thing today.

ANIMAL MYSTERIES

Not the least mystery is why they stuck with us this long. Really! And what they got for it besides tied out, starved, beaten, and neglected. Start with the big guys' majesty—elephants, rhinos, and dolphins. How they move. Whales who grew sick of the human comedy 50 million years ago and went back to the sea. Traded everything for ocean sleekness, yet they still seem to love us. How they roll and dive, and leap from the sea to fall back like rows of houses collapsing. Moving heaven and earth as the Bible says, and might add, "tumultuous waters surrounding." And birds' miracle of feathers—toucans, hummingbirds, peacocks— the wonder of sun-glazed wings, the intricacies of owl and warbler and chicken feather patterns and colors! Bugs, for some people. Fish, even snakes! Think of Burmese pythons glistening through the Everglades. Relax, they whisper in their slide-y way. We'll handle your dreams tonight. Then four-legged fur armies—horses, cats, rabbits, mice, zebra. Bears and buffalo and wolverines! Dogs who travel evolutionary trails all the way from Asian wolves to stare into our eyes. How they're able to focus on what's immediate—flies and ants, wind in tree leaves, invaders at the perimeter. They make concentration look as easy as reaction, stretching nose to tail and hair by hair matter-of-fact lovingly in a single motion that ties their edges and corners together into compact bundles itching to travel. How leaves move, they'd say, means at least as much as which way the wind blows. They'd tell us what they know, even how they know it, if we'd ask. If we knew how. The percheron's locomotive headlights of eye show that animals would gladly save humans if only we didn't insist that words mean less than their implications. Animals know the opposite is true. Wind means supper, wherever home turns out to be. Flowers mean spring. Water means life. Unashamed to sit alone in empty rooms containing their biggest thoughts merging and morphing, animals float more or less endlessly, drifting through voids of silence. Cairn terriers, for instance, flop down breathing accommodation out to their tail tips' last semaphore-flicks of consciousness. Then they curl into the shape of groans and blink their eyes marking us watching them as they fall into the sediments of sleep.

4

ELSEWHERE IN THE NOVEL

Servants polish the porcelain. The tea pot's tiny full moon shimmers. Cups and saucers gleam like barbs on bone fishhooks. Igor watches Helga's eyes shine above the circle of children. Buck teeth glow in the moonlight. Honed by ambition, Igor's breath catches on their fragility.

The duke in his three-piece corduroy suit seems resigned to patrol his greenhouse copse of dwarf trees. All these years later, he seems not to notice the limp marking the wound that changed his life. Birch trees caught in morning sunlight on the mountain slope tick with hoar frost.

Helga's eyes hold points of light like the wind picks out of water wrestling along the mill stream. Her family history wanders along the railroad track out of the foggy Caucasus on rope-soled sandals. One rail shines with rumor, the other glitters with possibility. They crinkle as though they're alive.

STORMS THAT CHANGE LIVES

Thunderstorms on Mt. Katahdin rattle Maine's tectonic plates. Odd-sized stacks of mountains—green, black, and white—surge all night through our sleep. The Moose Lodge tosses like a renegade ferryboat. Clinging to its rail, the President jabbers born-again code at parishioners in batty belfries. Splashed by lightning, Puritans flee serpentine insurrections. Mistress Bradstreet spits into her hands and digs in to lead off the last half of the ninth for the Scarlet Letters.

When morning finally comes, we wander the ocean shore's rich combination of new smells—bare roots, rye toast, reeking mud flats—all energyzed by the storm's ozone effect. We feel thinner, more focused. Something ominous seems forgiven. Horizons leap into the clear salt air, distinct wherever we look. Islands pop out of the water like surfacing loons. Friends lost for years swim back into memory. Surprise, stark as a loon's red eye, floats the water's rising flood.

MARKET DAY IN THE FAIRY TALE

Jugs of plum brandy, reliable elbows in any ear, wander the village crowd at dawn. The squeezebox grunts tunes everyone knows a few words of. Fresh wood smoke flavors the air. Men watch Emil's wife bend to the basket and stretch to hang wet wash on the line. They chew liver sausage and gnaw clay-colored pipe stems as they recall swimming naked as children. Pigs *oink* from their fenced-in corner. *How far we've come*, the squeezebox insists. Crosscut saws gnaw and iron wedges clank, insinuating their way. *Not for nothing*, pigs snort, *we've learned to eat our young.*

Time! the sackbut blares. Men grope wives and kiss babies. *Full bottles, please*, they chant. *And biscuits*, they pray. *Don't forget the sausage gravy.* Pigs wind along the path past Grandmother's house, picking their spots to dive into the forest. *Someone always knows the way*, they seem to say. Through the trees, castle towers hold threats of foreign war. *Edge of earth*, the squeezebox warns. *Mind what falls jagged from the sky.* The men shrug. They welcome any nap in the sun where their dream of naked supper always seems possible. *Whatever's next*, they whisper like a secret among themselves.

PATIENCE AND TERROR: AN OREGON TRAIL DOCUMENTARY

Imagine the walk west, each hand heavy
with all you can't bear
to leave. What's so important
to clench in each fist for two
thousand miles? Mostly tools. Axe
and hammer heads. Augers. Pliers to draw
molars, to hold nails sifted from fireplace ash
and hammer straight. Slates of family
Bible. Practical godliness thumbed suspender straps
and animal harness. Photographs,
daguerotypes, pens and ink

rode almost free.
Women's diaries named stretches of the trail
haunted by rotting animals and raw
excrement. They named what men ignored, or dared
not think. Dysentery, open graves, alkaline water,
wormy flour. Many men seemed lost, dazed
"by gigantic and enormous masses, a savage
sublimity of naked rock." But women
also proved vulnerable: "Disorder surrounds us
with a night picture of very wild
beauty." Photos show the strain

men bore. Their eyes drag with great effort
what they saw drift in the heat
and distance. "A melancholy strange-looking country—
one of fracture, violence, and fire." Add the mischief
of blown sand to everyday hazard, or clouds

burst with less warning than the appearance
of savages. Only Cap't Fremont's indispensable book
retained its bouyancy: "The pleasure of breathing
mountain air makes a constant theme of the hunter's praise
as if we had been drinking
exhilarating gas." Ox teams might walk

ten miles all day, the bulk of that way
driven sorely, or hauled at great bodily
expense. Compare bones to wheels
or axles, or wagon tongues. Which broke louder
on ears honed to what mattered
most? "Our setbacks render the company
silent." How soon other words appeared: "Full of ill-
will and little patience." Or:
"I walked off from the main party
and waited for the return of my
patience." Women did not walk

until their naiveté joined spinets
and virginals—failed furniture stacked
to daydream beside the trail. After childbirth
mothers wandered almost out of sight
guided by the quiet animals of their enormous
patience for moss swaddling and heirloom shreds
of meadowlark nest. "A stillness most profound,
and a terrible solitude" filled the scenes children—
their daughters and sons—received
as the new world's breath-
taking promise. Indians grew

from tall grass shadows at the speed

of gooseflesh. Black Night. Bad Bull's Tail—names
whose "wildness suited the character of people
who inhabit this country." How did the Indian
camps smell? What tiny clues fell
each day as women noticed their lives lose
more traces of home? What recognition dawned
the day a naked body caught
her glance? What tight-knuckled thought wrenched
her breath with her inkling that this place
will be home? Did she miss the balm of New

$ $ $

York lilac blossoms? Could she recall
the leisure they brought, the luxury of
shaded porches and the slow enchantment
of picnic afternoons? Could wagons—prairie camels!—
help
with their tricks of folding wheels to float
across streams, or sails spread to wander waves of grass
as prairie schooners? Once she gathered time
to think—her arms less and less numb from infant
demands—how did she bear her thought, grown
almost as full of wonder
as terror?

Safe beyond sister's picket fence-fantasy, brother's corporate expectations, and even mom's intuition, dad sees no chance of failure. What could go wrong? Shadows of conference tables turn furry and foreboding in night's tricky light? Not to worry. Wilderness surrounds us? Relax. Immensities happen. Keyboard-chatter sounds like rats scurrying through the shards of civilization? Twilight comes daily, dad says. But regardless, the market remains our shepherd.

Firing squads of Pliska, Bekarovka, and Schlivowicz take silent positions along the line strung between invisible and bullet-proof. What about difficult birth? Piffle. The kind of regret that leaves stains? Nothing makes dad flinch. He grins from spring's milky joints through gleaming ribs of longing. Opportunity surrounds us, he maintains. Each day's bridge to nowhere reaches satisfactory destinations. Hard as he studies what's unknown, there's not a deal-breaker in sight.

ERRATICS

Erratic: glacially transported rock

Most rocks squat like toads.
Some sprawl in weedy piles, numb
with groggy thought and sunning snake

eyebrows. Some stand on each other's shoulders,
blinded by balance until frost
knees them out of bed.

Odd rocks look like smoke
on Holstein hides, or furry
blizzard fronts. Erratics—fossils

the Indian glacier honed—
stand and face the wind they dare
to steal their cheekbones or sand

their callous knots smooth. Stray hearts,
erratics brood like Crazy Horse
off alone the night before

battle. Their pulses seethe
like fish sizzle in hot pans
enraged as they go.

SOMETHING HUMAN

What is it about the state
of our condition? *Please kick me
in the teeth* seems to follow us around
as though someone slapped a sign
on our backs. No matter the iron
taste of our blood, angels
diving like dreams from the sky
make us run crazy.
                        *Everything happens
for the best,* Mother said, smiling like a black hole
in the midnight sky. Didn't she show us how to twirl
our angel hair and turn screams
into cheers for the bundt cake
glazed with icy flames we sat
and shivered around? She always knew
what came down to what, even when soldiers
tumbled out of castle walls, feathers in
their caps and photos from home
in their pockets.
    *What has to be done
must always happen,* she said, rubbing
the hairy mole on her chin
for good luck. She clocked her shift early
that day of her funeral, remember,
to relax like holy men, content
on her bed of pointed nails.

LOST PHOTOS OF CRAZY HORSE

Fearlessness in battle gave his father the opportunity to rename him. The young man painted his face blue with white hailstones. Mixed an eagle's dried heart and brain with wild aster seeds hung in a pouch around his neck. Zig-zagged red earth from forehead to chin. Streaked his pony's fur and his own hair with dirt thrown by a burrowing mole whose blindness made them all harder to see. And so became Crazy Horse.

One day Indian agents gave him a knife and two cigars in a way that made him nervous. The flat rock he hung between his heart and the enemy grew cold.

Other days he sat with Assistant Army Surgeon Dr. Valentine T. McGillycuddy and smoked cigars. He refused the doctor's attempt to photograph him. *My bones will turn to rock after my death,* Crazy Horse said. *Why should you wish to shorten my life by taking from me my shadow?*

Take care of yourself, he told his friend Short Buffalo during a running skirmish with some Crows. *I'll do the fancy stunt.*

NIGHTS WHEN EVERYTHING WAITS

There's a night each of us wakes
somewhere inside of—a room
we'd never choose, so suddenly small
everything inside us bangs to leave.
Something out of sight has a smell

we realize we woke up
to escape. The sepia colored carpet's
tone of vague regret
reminds us of loss, spilled words
spread too thin too long

to take back. Her lips the night she left
locked like a frontier at war.
His arms tight across his chest
knit for shards big enough to
save, to hold and form and float

away on. The wallpaper pattern hints
that some wreckage waits
where we're headed. An answer's here
someplace, we keep thinking.
What's the question?

5

YOUTH

I vowed I'd quit ciggies on the heel of the mother
Of all hangovers. The world at noon pulsed a first

Columbus Ohio spring day. I'd fallen in love
Of course, as recently as chem lab and held

The ghost of her smell
In my clothes. Or lips

If I'd been lucky. My blood *thunk*
Thunk-thunked, the way a cut feels

As you bend to tie shoes. The way life
Tingles the first day it breaks loose

To crawl your skin. Dizzy,
I ran through milky sap and

Sycamore-leafed streets, mixing the smells
Of just-thawed earth with essence of girl

My blood steamed. I understood lost-at-sea as glamorous
Isolation, the way a hummingbird's movement through two

Eye blinks allows it to vanish and
Re-appear. My wings blurred hinges

Among worlds. Nothing held me. Nothing
Could catch me. I'd run this way forever.

CONSPIRACY 101

People who question the influence of Washington D.C. on everyday life help me recall fifth grade recess. We drew straws for who got to occupy the adults while one commando among us squeezed along a crawl space where a shed stood murky, fenced-off, and forbidden in one corner of the schoolyard. Safe out of sight, the lucky person searched out spider webs, snake dens, and trap doors that lead, our predecessors archived as rumors, deep into Civil War caverns. One day I found a seed company cap in the grass beside the shed. I left it lay (we knew not to disturb evidence!). The cap electrified my cohorts and confirmed our suspicions of a spy ring or weapons cache, or at least buried pirate treasure. (All orchestrated by Washington, we assumed. Why, we never asked.) Patriotism and wild speculation grew overnight. Were there pods? Was the alien invasion still on? I was stunned next day to see a janitor wearing the cap I'd found. An agent in overalls spit tobacco juice and washed the school blackboards? My mouth gaped, my hands shook. The man who swept floors was a spy, maybe a double agent! There were more inklings when our teacher broke into tears while reading us the last chapter of *Black Beauty* after recess just before the end of school. Why would anyone be sad when school ended, especially a teacher? Unless she was a double agent, or coerced by blackmail? Or maybe even a mole! The possibility left me faint. I spent the summer lost in speculation, compelled by what my dummy classmates ignored or overlooked. Even the most incriminating detail: On the day she couldn't go on, how did our teacher know who to pick to read in her place?

PORKBOMB

I dreamed of growing thin. At last
I put my feet down so hard fat pains
shook my world. I closed my ears
when grandma shrieked "Eat up!"
to keep my strength, smoothing my teddy-

bum with candied *this* and deep-
fried *that*. I resolved to eat only
for myself and walked away from fifty
pounds. I found my feet were distant relatives
with orderly kids. I grew small enough to spin

twin thoughts in my head at once
without bouncing off the earth at the whiff
bacon whispered, or anchovy pizza trolled
for survivors of breakfast. I grew so trim
I launched no waves in air, or wrenched

door frames I walked through, or slapped chairs silly,
astonished at my seat's force. At a hundred pounds
I couldn't stop dancing where I'd foundered
so often in the major food groups of grease,
sugar, and salt. My skin shrank so tight

I shivered to breathe. I began to live
my dreams. I felt valentines' subplots tickle
my crazy bones, jiggle my throat, and tease my
estrogen to simmer, steaming everything
I touched. The last fat clung deep as marrow

to my bones. I grew lean as apricots
or squads of milkweed seed crouched to spring
out of pods' dense holds. I flew like sparks
hummingbirds flash. I squiggled at last like a tadpole
of sperm, snug in my mother's egg at

sunrise. I slid through sunlight's zigzag
flight on water, quick as electricity turns
an atom's tight corner, calm as the core
of an echo. Calm enough for the first time
to decide what to do on my own.

LIVES OF THE ORDINARY LEAVES

Tiny lives break into sight and swell
our blood each spring, their cadence quick
as pulses. Boomtowns of leaves

roar out of taproots to flood
summer. Green banners swell
and billow the march down wide

bark boulevards. Autumn leaves swirl
mindless in the great letting
go. Brittle and overwhelmed,

the son's face in each leaf fills
his mother's eyes as
he finds himself home at last.

TWO CONSIDER THREE, WITH HOME, LOVE, JIM BEAM, AND LAST THINGS

One man thinks the whiskey smells like rain on gravel roads.

His friend recalls the home place. Barefoot picnics. Swinging on tires hung over the water. "Realtors?" Clouds of foreclosure drift through his voice. "A lawyer's glass eye blinks first."

 "No need to hold back," the first man says. Below the bottle's label, clear glass shows where purity begins. "How do you really feel?"

"Politicians?" his friend says. "Rather die in a ditch, I love this place so much."

ROSEMARY IN CLAY POTS

Rosemary plants in plain clay pots on window sills worn by ocean weather. Somehow they resemble bonsai, only less fastidious. Their branches look like old men's handfuls of stiff fingers. Nothing hurts, they say, long as we don't move.

Lavender-colored blossoms scatter among the rosemary leaves, splashes of color surprising more than beautiful. Like random leaks in galvanized milk buckets. Like children of parents with good will but too little imagination.

WHY I LOVE THE P.O.

Asians herd buffalo-sized crates to the counter. Chicanos kiss money goodbye they mail home. The line shakes heads at windows without clerks, shoulder shrugs, eyebrow twitches, and snorts all part of our dialect. *Anyone just dropping-off or picking-up?* I'm asked to translate. "That's not all of us?" I want to begin.

"Yo," a guy yells into his cell phone Wisconsin to Florida. "What zip you got there?"

Between me and my favorite clerk a jacket's faded embroidery reads *Corea*. "How much for a stamp in this man's world?" the jacket asks, buys, and tries to lick the self-stick peel. The clerk and I share a glance. I ask him what languages he needs for his job. "I talk English," he says. "And I talk smack. What's movin' today, Boss?"

ONE MORE THING THAT CAN'T BE SAID

They're friends so long they forget stories they share. Hunting stories. Life in the woods. Watching shadows, studying animal sign, predicting weather. Stillness. Silence. Expecting what comes.

Clichés slink around their canines. Euphemism thickens their tongues. Envy, and the ruins of unresolved jealousy. Each man feels certain he can stare through the picket fence-expression on his friend's face.

Their arms and legs gnarl into clubs and grow thick with animal hair. Neither man appears to notice the other's arm slide off the table and splash without ripples into the darkness between them.

TORN FROM HISTORY

Years before we watched Siam explode
into Thailand, we saw Nixon slither through McCarthy
Committee photos. Years after the Big One rocked
towns like Anzio and Tarawa, Tripoli and Pearl and Saipan—
ruins our uncles ransacked for stories to warn and thrill us—
mine stacked *Playboy*, the full run with Marilyn
on top. *Chick like that,* my uncle said to tell me he'd been
where I died to go. An Indiana doctor diagrammed bedroom-
mazes in *Life,* mazes where we safely wed-locked might
someday blunder. Frozen by indecision and mesmerized like bugs
in the syrup of exceptionalism, we vowed never
to be noticed until the morning we woke
famous. We clung to shiny fenders and bare
engines. Our flattop halos hovered like a squad of UFOs
trying to decide where was safe
to land among hunger pangs we barely
stood up under. Going-steady rings held us on paths
aimed at 2000, point of a double edge
no one could imagine growing old enough
to reach, and want to
survive. We saw *Picnic* a dozen times, watching Kim slide
far enough into our dreams to disconnect
our glittering spines. We hoped the stories were true:
what curled in her lap, all girl's laps, could steam us
pure. We hoped until we felt our knees shiver
to jelly. We tried to stand. Then we learned
to pray. Those were the years
we took up prayer for life.

Notes & Acknowledgements

NOTES

"Pitching Horseshoes" and "Two Consider Three, with Home, Love, Jim Beam, and Last Things": Dedicated to Dan Bell.

GreatPlains: In addition to the 2002 Red Dragonfly Press edition of *GreatPlains: A Prairie Lovesong*, Michael Koppa made a wonderful small press book called "Native Son At Home" composed of six sections of GreatPlains with his own illustrations in 2000 at his Heavy Duty Press in St. Francis, Wisconsin.

"What Farm Boys Say When They Have to Talk": Dedicated to Jack Miller and Jerry Bourquin.

"Drunk on American Mythology": Dedicated to Tim Black.

"My Famous Classmate": Every other bartender and their biographers seem to offer interpretations of the famous personality. But as a lifelong Midwest resident I grew up with a dozen similar personalities. Much insight also is on display at the Hemingway Foundation in Oak Park, Illinois.

"Dreams-on-His-Skin": The National Gallery of Art could come no closer to the artist who painted "Prize Bull" in 1876 than "H. Call." I therefor felt free to invent the artist's personality.

"Up in Wisconsin": Much language I've heard at Wisconsin farm auctions, bars, and gas stations is a joy to remember and repeat. One guy held my oil dipstick up to the car window and said, "I give her a couple shots. She's up there nice and clean" as though he were reading lines from a poem.

"Great Ghosts": Luna moths, walking sticks, barn owls, caddis fly larvae. These and other surprising pure products of the rural Midwest provided me awe and inspiration.

"Renaming the Warblers": Blossom Dearie, the jazz singer of "Little Jazz Bird."

"Snapping Turtle": Dedicated to Franco Pagnucci and his book *Ancient Moves*.

"Midwest Café Dialog, with Dogs and Horses": Robert Bly's discussions about Midwestern conversation made me start listening closely to vernacular language.

"Photos of Alaskan Bears": Dedicated to Toby Sherry.

"Storms That Change Lives": The Green Mountains of Vermont, the Black Mountains of Maine, the White Mountains of New Hampshire.

"America's Century": I heard the image of scurrying rats in a lecture delivered by Alexander Cockburn.

"Patience and Terror: An Oregon Trail Documentary": Quotations and many details come from J.C. Fremont's *Narrative of the Exploring Expedition to the Rocky Mountains in the Year 1842* (known as the *Homesteader's Indispensable Guide*), and from Lillian Schlissel's *Women's Diaries of the Westward Journey*, 1982.

"The Lost Photos of Crazy Horse": My favorite book on this and similar subjects is Ian Frazier's *Great Plains* which includes 65 pages of notes and book citations.

"Torn from History": Nominated for a Pushcart Prize, 2015.

ACKNOWLEDGEMENTS

Some of these poems have previously appeared in the following publications, often in different versions with other titles, to whose editors grateful acknowledgement is made.

Magazines: *Abraxas, Beloit Poetry Journal, Arttimes Wisconsin, Clockwatch Review, The Galley Sail Review, The Great River Review, LakeCityLights.com, Mid-American Review, Nimrod, North Dakota Quarterly, The North American Review, Northeast, The Ohio Review, Poetry, Poetry Motel, Poetry Northwest, River Styx, Seems, Spoon River Quarterly, Transactions, Verse Wisconsin, Wisconsin Academy Review, Wisconsin Poets' Calendar, Wisconsin Review, Wisconsin Trails*, and *Yahara Review*.

Anthologies: *Contemporary Poetry in America*, ed. Miller Williams, 1989; *Echolocations: Poets Map Madison*, ed. By Sarah Busse, Shoshauna Shy, and Wendy Vardeman, 2013; *Face the Poem*, ed. Franco Pagnucci, 1982; *From the Tongue of the Crow: Wisconsin Review 25th Anniversary Anthology*, 1987; *Heartland II*, ed. Lucien Stryk, 1975; *The Journey Home: The Literature of Wisconsin through Four Centuries*, ed. Jim Stephens, 1989; *Keys to the Interior: Twenty-Five Years of Great River Review*, ed. Richard Broderick and Robert Hedin, 2002; *Low Down and Coming On: Poems About Pigs*, ed. James P. Lenfesty, 2010; *Perfect Dragonfly: Fifteen Years of Red Dragonfly Press Publishing*, ed. Scott King, 2011; and *Vital Signs: Contemporary American Poetry from the University Presses*, ed. Ron Wallace, 1989.

Several "New" poems in this book appeared for the first time in these magazines:

Abraxas: "Great Ghosts."
Apalachee Quarterly: "Porkbomb."
Echolocations: Poets Map Madison: "Animal Effigy Mounds."
Great River Review: "Erratics," " A Glimpse into the Old World," "Torn from History," "Two Red Bellied Woodpecker Tail Feathers," "Undressing the Scarecrow."
LakeCityPoets.com: "Bigfoot's Back in Town," "Conspiracy 101," "Honeymoon," "New Orleans Parades," "Storms That Change Lives," "What Farm Boys Say When They Have to Talk," "Why I Love the P.O."
Perfect in Their Art: Poems About Boxing from Homer to Ali: "Monster."
Poetry: "Nights When Everything Waits."
Seems: "One More Thing That Can't Be Said," "Midwest Cafe Dialog, with Dogs and Horses," "Two Consider Three, with Home, Love, Jim Beam, and Last Things."
Shepherd's Express Online: "Photos of Alaskan Bears."
Verse Wisconsin: "America's Century," "Up in Wisconsin."
Yahara Poetry Review: "Hugging A President Who Talks Tough."

ABOUT THE AUTHOR

Hunt & Gather is David's seventh book of poems, the one he likes most, and the first to concern itself with prose poems. He never thought much about prose poems until he had so much trouble casting a certain poem into lines that he decided to try it as prose. The idea now, after several years, is not to worry about line breaks but instead to concentrate on developing arresting imagery and as compelling a flow of attractive language as possible. He lives and writes in Madison, Wisconsin

Made in the USA
San Bernardino, CA
25 October 2016